DAY BY DAY

A CREATIVE GUIDE TO LIVING YOUR BEST LIFE
WITH CLARITY, INTENTION & FLOW

AMY MEYER

Day By Day
A Creative Guide to Living Your Best Life with Clarity, Intention & Flow

ISBN: 9781096302032

For more, visit www.TheSoulShineCollective.com
or email thesoulshinecollective@gmail.com

Dedication

This journal is dedicated to the souls who know they are capable of
so much more, but feel overwhelmed and have no idea how to get there.
I created this guide for you because I was you.
From my heart to yours, I understand.
My soul sees and honors the light in yours.
Trust that day by day, you will get there.
Enjoy the journey.

Contents

Welcome from the Author 6

Ground & Center Meditation 8

Prayer / Intention 9

How To Make the Most of This Experience 10

· Daily Pages & Weekly Soul Check ·

Week One 22

Week Two 60

Week Three 98

Week Four 136

· Extras ·

Creative Affirmation Pages 174

Clear the Clutter & Free Your Soul Challenge 206

Dig Deep Journal Prompts 212

Welcome from the Author...

Welcome to the next day of your beautiful life and soul journey! You are here on purpose and it is my ultimate pleasure and honor to be a part of it.

I am a creative soul and I have the innate ability to connect with people before I even know anything about them. For most of my life, I didn't allow this natural gift to work through me; I instead resisted it and I had no idea what to do with the energy. This misunderstood gift, combined with my husband's unexpected open heart surgery at age 30 (when our first born was only seven months old), postpartum depression after my second child, losing my 11-year-old fur baby, balancing mommy-hood, a full-time job, building my photography business, struggling with co-dependency, denial, emotional eating and drinking, and finally hitting rock bottom, that I decided enough was enough. I remember the moment clearly and in that moment I decided to begin my healing and wellness journey.

I realized that I had to put one foot in front of the other, trusting that day by day, things would improve and I knew I had the light within me to arrive at that place. Trusting and believing that truth and ultimately realizing in order to feel aligned and free, I had to come center and release the need to control. I had to be consistent, day by day, in doing these daily and weekly rituals so that I could stand in my own power.

And I also realized that when it comes our journeys here on Earth, there is no one way that works for everyone. Recognizing that was freeing for me and I hope it resonates with you as well. I created this guide for you because I know through experience that I am not alone in these struggles.

Welcome from the Author...

It is my honor and pleasure to share with you a small glimpse of the rituals and tools I have used through the years to get to a place of flow instead of force. As you can imagine, this flow didn't happen overnight, but day by day, step by step, one inspired action at a time, life began to flow. It is a daily practice, and just like the waves in the ocean, there are ebbs and flow, but I am now armed with the tools, rituals and mindset to get through the struggles.

Use this guide as your soul leads you. As you are working through it, keep in mind that there are no wrong answers and that your journey is your own. Honor that truth. Hold space for yourself. Step away as you need to. Breathe. Scribe, doodle and brainstorm as you feel inspired. This guide is not meant to fix anything about you. You are a perfectly imperfect human and so incredibly beautiful! This guide is meant to take you on a journey of creating healthy habits and rituals to live your most abundant life, with clarity, intention and in alignment with who you are here to be. Take it day by day and do what you know and feel is right.
It is up to you. The answers are within. Trust that.

Remember, the way you do one thing is the way you do all things. Commit to doing the daily pages and dedicate a few minutes each day to check in with your soul. Trust that the magic will happen when you go all in. Feel free to do all of the prompts daily, or do only the prompts you feel led to do. But do something. It will change your life. Guaranteed.

I am grateful for you and cannot wait to hear how this helps you. I see the light within you and am so honored to be here. At the end of the day, we are one, we are the light and I am honored to journey with you.

Blessings & Love to You,
Amy

Ground & Center

Feel free to use this exercise as you begin your day (or anytime!)
Audio version: https://thesoulshinecollective.com/day-by-day-a-creative-guide-to-living-your-best-life-with-clarity-intention-flow/
[Case Sensitive] Password: daybyday

Shut off all distractions.
Get comfortable.
Light a candle, diffuse your favorite essential oil, dim the lights,
grab your favorite pen & a beverage of choice.

Close your eyes.

Inhale... take a deep breath ... 1-2-3-4

And hold for 4-3-2-1

Release ... let it out.
And inhale 1-2-3-4 ...

And hold for 4-3-2-1 ...

Release. Let it out.

Repeat until you feel calm and centered.

You might find yourself wanting to pray, meditate or repeat your affirmation.
Do what feels good.

You may want to journal. If so, go for it! When you feel centered, allow your pen to flow. Don't overthink, don't force. Just let it flow.

If you need to step away and come back, do so. It will be in your best interest so you'll be in a state of flow. Enjoy!

Prayer / Intention

Feel free to use this suggested prayer or create your own meditation, prayer or intention here. Or make a list of your favorites so you can refer back to them. Make it your own so it resonates with your soul!

Audio version: https://thesoulshinecollective.com/day-by-day-a-creative-guide-to-living-your-best-life-with-clarity-intention-flow/
[Case Sensitive] Password: daybyday

Dear God/Universe/Source/Higher Power:

I believe I am confident.
I believe I am capable.
I love myself and believe in myself.
I believe I am enough.
Please guide me through this journey of
discovery and show me grace and peace to my soul.
Help me break free and accept who I am.
Please help me release judgement of myself and others as I work
through this guide, day by day.
I allow my thoughts and my pen to flow as you move through me.
Thank you.
And so it is.
Amen.

How to make the most of this experience...

How To Use This Journal

However you feel led. There is no right or wrong way. I created this guide based on habits I have created and what works for me. I offer suggestions for each section.

Disclaimer: I am not a therapist or doctor and am simply sharing habits that have worked for me. Always listen to your body and seek the advice of a professional as needed.

Weekly Intentions

Get still before the start of each week. I suggest sitting in silence, play soothing meditation music or your favorite pump up jams - whatever helps you get grounded and centered. Make this journal your own. Make it work for you. Acknowledge your desires and enjoy the process and flow of your writing. Draw, doodle, paint, get creative as you wish. Ask yourself how you want to feel and set your intentions. Always let your soul guide you and know that you are worthy of it all.

At the beginning of each week, you will find a "weekly intentions" section. Here you will find these two questions:

1) How do you want to feel this week? and
2) What are you going to be intentional about this week?

You will also find a list of words and free space to write. Do what you will with this section. Suggestions: Circle the words you feel drawn to, commit to setting intentions based on those desired words. Doodle on them, create reminders on your phone to bring yourself back to these desires. Create affirmations from them. Journal on the words you choose. Write the words several times and feel into them. It is truly up to you. Listen to what your soul is calling you to and own it!

Free Write

Suggestions:

Fill this space with your desires, your intentions, prayers, affirmation, your to-do list, your to-don't list. Use it to brain dump all the things you need to do so you can create a list of priorities for the week. Doodle or draw. Get creative. It's your space.

Weekly Challenge:

At the beginning of each week, you will find a weekly challenge. The purpose of the challenge is to help you cultivate a practice that feels good. These challenges are meant to nudge you out of your comfort zone. Enjoy the ride and don't stress over any of them - again there is no right or wrong way to do these. Make it fun!

Suggestions:
Involve your family, spouse or a friend. Doing so provides a space
for connection and accountability. Make it fun!

How to make the most of this experience...

Daily Pages

You will find ☼ symbols at the top of every page with the following words: breathe, hydrate, move and soul care. These are meant to be checked off upon completion daily. These are habits that I have created and have helped heal me over the years. My intention is that they help you as well. Remember, use these as they resonate with you. Don't stress if the box isn't checked daily. Do what works for you, based on your intentions and your soul's needs.

☼ BREATHE

We all lead such busy lives that we struggle to stop and simply breathe and be present in the moment. Living is breathing and when we find a few minutes out of our day to appreciate that, we feel more relaxed, grateful and abundant. Spend some time in meditation/prayer or simply sitting in stillness taking deep breaths.

Suggestions:

Breathe in your nose for four breaths, hold for seven seconds, and release out your mouth for eight seconds. (4-7-8) Doing this exercise has been proven to release tension and anxiety and it has saved me many times in my journey when I feel overwhelmed, anxious, stressed or out of control.
You can find a plethora of free meditation apps. If you are new to meditation, I suggest first trying a guided meditation that's 10 minutes or less.

☼ HYDRATE

Drink your water! Water flushes toxins, increases energy, improves skin, promotes weight loss, boosts the immune system, and helps aid in digestion.

Suggestions:

I drink at least half my body weight in ounces daily, more when it's hot or when I do strenuous exercise. Listen to your body. Set a goal for yourself and check the sun when you've met it! I will often add lemon, lime, raspberries or oranges to my water. It is refreshing and has added benefits. Bonus: I don't get bored with plain water.

MOVE

Move your body daily. It helps relieve stress, energizes, and boosts confidence. It will raise your vibes instantly and get the endorphins flowing. The hardest part is starting, but once you do, you are unstoppable. Just start!

Suggestions:

We all have a few minutes a day to move, even if it's stretching at your desk, doing a few push ups in between commercials, or a dance party just because! Just do it, you'll feel better! Number one tip I can give you is to find something you enjoy and do it! I honestly love most all types of exercise and over the years have found that my body will tell me what it needs, whether it's yoga, running, HIIT workouts, weightlifting, gymnastics or all of the above. Your body will tell you too, you just have to listen, start and then be consistent. You are powerful!

 SOUL CARE

Did you take some time for you?

Suggestions:

Read, call a friend, listen to a podcast that lights you up, do something creative, sit in nature, straighten your creative space, enjoy a lunch date with someone you haven't seen in a while, do one thing off your Soul Shine list (the Week One Challenge).

Whatever you decide, be sure it lights you up and leaves you feeling full of joy, peace and love.

How to make the most of this experience...

Daily Pages

You will find the same prompts and create lists each day. Some days may be the same as the others. Remember, there is no one way, right way or wrong way to do these activities. The intention is to create these habits that will move you into a space of living with intention, in gratitude and flow.

How I Want to Feel Today...

Write the first thing that comes to your mind. Trust your soul on this. You don't have to explain it, just feel it. And remember that you are worthy of all your desires!

I Am _____...

I am is one of the most powerful statements we can say. Our thoughts create our reality. By speaking these statements out loud daily, feeling them, believing them, over time our lives will change and the thoughts will become our reality.

Each day, write an affirmation (or more if you like!) to carry you through. You might choose to focus and say the same one every day for that week, or the entire length of this journal. You may have a different one daily. It is up to you. Whatever you do, the most important part of writing the affirmations is that you feel them as you write them, repeating believe them as if they were already true. Because they are.

Suggestions:

Write these, speak them out loud, set them as alarms or reminders on your phone, create sticky notes, put them on your mirrors, computer, anywhere you will see them daily and often.

Bonus! I have created Creative Affirmation Pages in the back of this workbook - feel free to use those affirmations as they resonate with you.

Another way is to take a negative thought you may be struggling with and flip the script. Turn it into an affirmation. *For example*: "I feel so unmotivated and sad today." Your affirmation could be: "I am strong, capable and full of joy!"

How to make the most of this experience...

Three Things I'm Grateful For...

Practicing gratitude opens our hearts and the universe to create space for our desires. On your list, list the little things, the big things, the things that haven't happened yet that you are calling in, whatever you are ever so grateful for. Try to list different things each day.

Examples:

my family, our health, my job, sunshine through my windows, cup of hot coffee, sound of my children's laughter, the hum of the refrigerator and the food that it holds, the sound of the birds outside, etc.

Three Things I Love About Myself...

Self awareness, self love and self worth go hand in hand. I struggled with self love for a number of years, but until I became aware of it, and believed I was worthy, I stayed in a cycle of self destruction and habits that did not serve my highest good. Society, social media, negative people in our lives, and our environment can all be detrimental to our self love and confidence. Recognizing that we are love and light and worthy just because we are is so freeing and so magical!

I encourage you to dig deep and find three different things that you love about yourself daily. These can be anything - please don't focus only on the physical.

Examples: I love that I see potential in everyone I meet and meet them with compassion instead of judgment. I love my eyes. I love my sense of style. I love that I am a wonderful mom. I love that I am determined.

I understand that this portion may be a struggle for some, depending on where you are in your journey and that is okay. Do not judge yourself for feeling this way. If you're struggling with this exercise, I encourage you to get still, meditate or pray and ask your higher power to show you what is wonderful about you. And then listen. It may be easy to judge what comes through, but replace those judgmental thoughts with an affirmation. Enjoy this practice.

You are beautiful just as you are and so worthy!

How to make the most of this experience...

Three Things I Have To Do Today...

List the things that you don't want to do but must get done today. I don't know about you, but I often put off the things that I dread that if I would just do them, I would feel lighter and it allows me to focus on the things that I need to do without stressing too much.

Examples:
Making that phone call, paying a bill, cleaning the bathroom, taking the movie back, having that uncomfortable conversation, scheduling the meeting, etc. I have found that if I put my "musts" - the things that absolutely have to get done for the day on this list, then the other to-do's are easier to focus on and finish.

Three Things I Won't Do Today...

List the things you won't do today. Boundaries and protecting your energy are important in living a life on purpose and in flow. It also might be a goal you're trying to meet and you can list anything that may hinder this goal. Remember, none of this is set in stone and can be ever evolving, so be sure to give yourself grace.

Examples:
Allow others to offend me.
Allow things to distract me from my purpose.
Ignore my boundaries.
I will not have a soda today.
I will not scroll social media mindlessly today.

How to make the most of this experience...

My Soul Is Calling Me To...

One of the most powerful tools I have found on my own personal growth journey is the power of free writing. This prompt is one I use often and every time I feel uninspired or stuck.

Suggestion:

Get still, turn off distractions and play some soothing music. Close your eyes and ask your soul and higher power to write through you, leading with love, compassion and purpose. Set a timer for 4-6 minutes and let your pen flow. The most important thing is to not judge, not edit and not think. Allow whatever comes through to come through. When the timer goes off, read through what you wrote. You may feel the desire to write more. Feel free to continue, trusting and knowing that you are being divinely led.

Desires...

Some of these desires may come from the *My Soul is Calling Me To* prompt or they may come from your weekly intentions list. These can be anything that rings true for you, big or small. Remember, it is important not to judge these desires and to trust that they are where your higher power and your soul are leading you.

Examples:

Drink more water, commit to calling my sister once a week, date night with my husband once a month, extra play time with my kids, write a book, open my own clothing store, exercise three times this week...you get the idea.

How to make the most of this experience...

Inspired Action Steps I Will Take Today...

When we feel inspired and led, we are in flow and we put in the work to create things and make them happen. To chase our dreams and desires. It is impossible to build a house in a day, but day by day, brick by brick, layer by layer, piece by piece, it starts to take shape. The purpose of this prompt is to guide you to create one (just one!) action step that you will take today to get you closer to your desire.

Step by step, action by action, day by day.

I am a dreamer and a creative, so my mind often wanders and thinks so big that I have to rein it back. If I don't, then the idea becomes too overwhelming and then the worst thing happens... Nothing. I cannot tell you how many times in my past I have allowed the fear of the big picture to paralyze me. Maybe this resonates with you, and if so, this activity will help you.

Examples:
Desire: Write a book.
Action Step: Schedule uninterrupted time to write 2,500 pages today.

Desire: Drink more water.
Action Step: Purchase pretty water bottle to keep me inspired and use it!

Free Write

Simply extra space for you to spill your heart. Use it however you wish. Write, doodle, draw, stamp... it is your space. Use sticky notes, photos, quotes, draw, color, make lists, etc. Whatever you are led to create and use in this space.

Suggestions:
Check in at the end of the day. How do you feel? Did you complete your desires? Make another gratitude list. Take notes. Brain dump your to-do list for the next day. Write your meal plan ideas or recipes you want to try.

How to make the most of this experience...

Weekly Soul Check & Free Write Pages

These questions are meant to push you out of your comfort zone, dig deep and create ways to call in more positive and feelings of flow. You may find you need extra space and I have included a few extra pages just for that as well as any other things you may want to expand upon.

Examples:
Brain dump all the things you have to do, are happy with, grateful for, celebrate this week and all your wins!

You are amazing!

I Am / Creative Affirmation Pages

Use these pages to let your mind wander, color, doodle, outline, create your art surrounding it. When you're finished, take a photo of the page and save to your desktop or your phone. Rip these pages out and post them where you can see them. Frame them. Use them however you wish. Own it and make it yours!

Clear the Clutter & Free Your Soul Challenge

These mini-challenges are meant to help you clear the clutter in your environment and your mind. You may decide to tackle one mini challenge at a time or pick a few to do each day. Use the sun as a check box if you like. Schedule reminders on your phone with the challenges that resonate. As always, use these as you wish and have fun with them!

Dig Deep Journal Prompts

These prompts are a collection of prompts that have helped me along my own journey and it is my intention and prayer that they help you as well. Some of the questions will challenge you, may trigger you and will definitely push you beyond your comfort zone. If at any time you feel overwhelmed or triggered, I recommend stepping away and saying a prayer or setting an intention based on your feelings and needs. And come back to the question as you feel led. Some of the prompts may resonate with you, others may not. Take what does and use it as you will and leave the rest. Enjoy these and visit them as often as you need to. It is important not to judge your feelings and emotions or your answers. Trust and know that whatever you're feeling is what you're supposed to feel. Recognize and accept your feelings and answer the prompts without judgement. It will help you move through exactly what you need to. You are being divinely led and this is a beautiful journey.

Enjoy!

Week One

. . .

Breathe

Weekly Intentions

Dates: _____

How do you want to feel this week? What are you going to be intentional about this week?

Calm	Trusting	Forgiven
Flow	Aligned	Free
Unapologetic	Happy	Valued
Healthy	Enough	Heard
Anchored	Guided	Seen
Focused	Recharged	Loved

Weekly Challenge

Create a Soul Shine List.

What makes your soul shine and your heart soar?
What lights you up? What makes you feel joyful and on top of the world?
What gives you chills and what keeps you going? Dig deep into this challenge.
Make time to enjoy a few things off your list at least once this week.

Date: _____ M T W Th F S Su

☀ BREATHE   ☀ HYDRATE   ☀ MOVE   ☀ SOUL CARE

Trust yourself.

How I want to feel today:

_____

I am:

_____

Three things I'm grateful for:

1) _____
   _____
2) _____
   _____
3) _____
   _____

Three things I love about myself:

1) _____
   _____
2) _____
   _____
3) _____
   _____

Three things I have to do today:

1) _____
   _____
2) _____
   _____
3) _____
   _____

Three things I won't do today:

1) _____
   _____
2) _____
   _____
3) _____
   _____

My soul is calling me to.....

Desire(s):

_____

_____

_____

_____

Inspired Action Step(s) I will take today:

_____

_____

_____

_____

Free Write

Date: _____ M T W Th F S Su

○ BREATHE   ○ HYDRATE   ○ MOVE   ○ SOUL CARE

Just be.

How I want to feel today:

_____

I am:

_____

Three things I'm grateful for:

1) _____
   _____
2) _____
   _____
3) _____
   _____

Three things I love about myself:

1) _____
   _____
2) _____
   _____
3) _____
   _____

Three things I have to do today:

1) _____
   _____
2) _____
   _____
3) _____
   _____

Three things I won't do today:

1) _____
   _____
2) _____
   _____
3) _____
   _____

My soul is calling me to .....

Desire(s):

_____

_____

_____

Inspired Action Step(s) I will take today:

_____

_____

_____

Free Write

Date: _____ M T W Th F S Su

☼ BREATHE   ☼ HYDRATE   ☼ MOVE   ☼ SOUL CARE

When you know, you know.

How I want to feel today:

_____

I am:

_____

Three things I'm grateful for:

1) _____

_____

2) _____

_____

3) _____

_____

Three things I love about myself:

1) _____

_____

2) _____

_____

3) _____

_____

Three things I have to do today:

1) _____

_____

2) _____

_____

3) _____

_____

Three things I won't do today:

1) _____

_____

2) _____

_____

3) _____

_____

My soul is calling me to ....

Desire(s):

_____

_____

_____

Inspired Action Step(s) I will take today:

_____

_____

_____

Free Write

Date: _____ M T W Th F S Su

☼ BREATHE   ☼ HYDRATE   ☼ MOVE   ☼ SOUL CARE

One step at a time.

How I want to feel today:

_____

I am:

_____

Three things I'm grateful for:

1) _____
   _____
2) _____
   _____
3) _____
   _____

Three things I love about myself:

1) _____
   _____
2) _____
   _____
3) _____
   _____

Three things I have to do today:

1) _____
   _____
2) _____
   _____
3) _____
   _____

Three things I won't do today:

1) _____
   _____
2) _____
   _____
3) _____
   _____

My soul is calling me to .....

Desire(s):

_____

_____

_____

Inspired Action Step(s) I will take today:

_____

_____

_____

Free Write

Date: _____   M T W Th F S Su

☼ BREATHE   ☼ HYDRATE   ☼ MOVE   ☼ SOUL CARE

Live your truth.

How I want to feel today:

_____

I am:

_____

Three things I'm grateful for:

1) _____
   _____
2) _____
   _____
3) _____
   _____

Three things I love about myself:

1) _____
   _____
2) _____
   _____
3) _____
   _____

Three things I have to do today:

1) _____
   _____
2) _____
   _____
3) _____
   _____

Three things I won't do today:

1) _____
   _____
2) _____
   _____
3) _____
   _____

My soul is calling me to .....

Desire(s):

_____
_____
_____

Inspired Action Step(s) I will take today:

_____
_____
_____

Free Write

Date: _____ M T W Th F S Su

☼ BREATHE   ☼ HYDRATE   ☼ MOVE   ☼ SOUL CARE

Immerse yourself in wonder.

How I want to feel today:

_____

I am:

_____

Three things I'm grateful for:

1) _____
_____
2) _____
_____
3) _____
_____

Three things I love about myself:

1) _____
_____
2) _____
_____
3) _____
_____

Three things I have to do today:

1) _____
_____
2) _____
_____
3) _____
_____

Three things I won't do today:

1) _____
_____
2) _____
_____
3) _____
_____

My soul is calling me to.....

Desire(s):

_____
_____
_____
_____

Inspired Action Step(s) I will take today:

_____
_____
_____
_____

Date: _____ M T W Th F S Su

☼ BREATHE   ☼ HYDRATE   ☼ MOVE   ☼ SOUL CARE

Embrace who you are becoming.

How I want to feel today:

_____

I am:

_____

Three things I'm grateful for:

1) _____

_____

2) _____

_____

3) _____

_____

Three things I love about myself:

1) _____

_____

2) _____

_____

3) _____

_____

Three things I have to do today:

1) _____

_____

2) _____

_____

3) _____

_____

Three things I won't do today:

1) _____

_____

2) _____

_____

3) _____

_____

My soul is calling me to .....

Desire(s):

_____

_____

_____

Inspired Action Step(s) I will take today:

_____

_____

_____

Weekly Soul Check

Describe how you felt this week in one word:

_____

If it was positive feeling, what can you do to feel that way more often?

_____

If it was a negative feeling, what can you do to feel more positive?

_____

What am I forcing?

_____

What am I allowing?

_____

What is one thing I will do less of?

_____

What is one thing I will do more of?

_____

What didn't work this week?

_____

I am releasing:

_____

I am calling in:

_____

Celebrate! What went well this week?

_____

Trust yourself.

Just be.

When you know, you know.

One step at a time.

Live your truth.

Immerse yourself in
wonder.

Embrace who you are
becoming.

Week Two
...
CreateSpace

Weekly Intentions

Dates: _____

How do you want to feel this week? What are you going to be intentional about this week?

Inspired	Creative	Safe
Focused	Joyful	Nourished
Relaxed	Surrendered	Selfless
Mindful	Grateful	Magnetic
Authentic	Understood	Alive
Passionate	Fierce	Shining

Weekly Challenge
Get Outside / Log Off & Out

Get outside. A quick and easy way to hit reset on mindset and life is to
get outside for some fresh air and natural light. Challenge yourself to be
100 percent present with yourself, your family, significant other, and/or friends.

Suggestions:
- Set your phone and other devices to airplane mode or turn off.
- Journal any feelings and thoughts that come to you.
- Breathe in the air around you.
- Look up at the sky, observe the clouds, feel the sun on your face.
- Remove your shoes, feel the earth beneath your feet.
- Ground yourself.
Breathe in for four seconds. Hold for seven. Release for eight seconds.
- Let go. Relax. Enjoy.

Journal Prompts:
How did you feel to get out?
How did you feel to be present with yourself? With your family/spouse/friends?
Do you get outside often?
How did it feel to let go?
Did you feel something inside you shift or stir?
Do you plan to do this more often?

Weekly Challenge:

Let go of negativity and things that no longer serve you.

Negativity breeds negativity and your mind is a powerful tool.
If you don't feed it with good things, it will perish.

Suggestions:
Do a walk through of your house and throw away old receipts, trash, paperwork, etc.
Clean out your closet - make a pile for trash, donate, sell and then follow through.
Clean out your purse. It's amazing how freeing that feels!
Make a list of things/people/circumstances/beliefs/anything
that is no longer serving your highest good and why. Replace the things you list with positive
affirmations or thoughts. Review the list daily to keep you focused on moving forward.

Journal Prompts:
How does it feel to release the negativity?
How does it feel to get rid of the extra energy/physical things/ that no
longer serves your highest good?
Do you feel refreshed, lighter, at peace?

Date: _____ M T W Th F S Su

☀ BREATHE   ☀ HYDRATE   ☀ MOVE   ☀ SOUL CARE

Be still.

How I want to feel today:

_____

I am:

_____

Three things I'm grateful for:

1) _____
   _____
2) _____
   _____
3) _____
   _____

Three things I love about myself:

1) _____
   _____
2) _____
   _____
3) _____
   _____

Three things I have to do today:

1) _____
   _____
2) _____
   _____
3) _____
   _____

Three things I won't do today:

1) _____
   _____
2) _____
   _____
3) _____
   _____

My soul is calling me to.....

Desire(s):

_____

_____

_____

Inspired Action Step(s) I will take today:

_____

_____

_____

Free Write...

Free Write

Date: _____   M T W Th F S Su

:Ò: BREATHE   :Ò: HYDRATE   :Ò: MOVE   :Ò: SOUL CARE

Silence the noise.

How I want to feel today:

_____

I am:

_____

Three things I'm grateful for:

1) _____
_____
2) _____
_____
3) _____
_____

Three things I love about myself:

1) _____
_____
2) _____
_____
3) _____
_____

Three things I have to do today:

1) _____
_____
2) _____
_____
3) _____
_____

Three things I won't do today:

1) _____
_____
2) _____
_____
3) _____
_____

My soul is calling me to .....

Desire(s):

Inspired Action Step(s) I will take today:

Date: _____ M T W Th F S Su

☼ BREATHE   ☼ HYDRATE   ☼ MOVE   ☼ SOUL CARE

Let it be.

How I want to feel today:

_____

I am:

_____

Three things I'm grateful for:

1) _____
   _____
2) _____
   _____
3) _____
   _____

Three things I love about myself:

1) _____
   _____
2) _____
   _____
3) _____
   _____

Three things I have to do today:

1) _____
   _____
2) _____
   _____
3) _____
   _____

Three things I won't do today:

1) _____
   _____
2) _____
   _____
3) _____
   _____

My soul is calling me to.....

Desire(s):

Inspired Action Step(s) I will take today:

Date: _____ M T W Th F S Su

☼ BREATHE   ☼ HYDRATE   ☼ MOVE   ☼ SOUL CARE

Choose again.

How I want to feel today:

_____

I am:

_____

Three things I'm grateful for:

1) _____

_____

2) _____

_____

3) _____

_____

Three things I love about myself:

1) _____

_____

2) _____

_____

3) _____

_____

Three things I have to do today:

1) _____

_____

2) _____

_____

3) _____

_____

Three things I won't do today:

1) _____

_____

2) _____

_____

3) _____

_____

My soul is calling me to.....

Desire(s):

_____
_____
_____

Inspired Action Step(s) I will take today:

_____
_____
_____

Date: _____   M T W Th F S Su

☼ BREATHE   ☼ HYDRATE   ☼ MOVE   ☼ SOUL CARE

Savor the moments.

How I want to feel today:

_____

I am:

_____

Three things I'm grateful for:

1) _____
   _____
2) _____
   _____
3) _____
   _____

Three things I love about myself:

1) _____
   _____
2) _____
   _____
3) _____
   _____

Three things I have to do today:

1) _____
   _____
2) _____
   _____
3) _____
   _____

Three things I won't do today:

1) _____
   _____
2) _____
   _____
3) _____
   _____

My soul is calling me to .....

Desire(s):

_____

_____

_____

Inspired Action Step(s) I will take today:

_____

_____

_____

Free Write

Date: _____ M T W Th F S Su

☀ BREATHE   ☀ HYDRATE   ☀ MOVE   ☀ SOUL CARE

You are magic.

How I want to feel today:

_____

I am:

_____

Three things I'm grateful for:

1) _____

_____

2) _____

_____

3) _____

_____

Three things I love about myself:

1) _____

_____

2) _____

_____

3) _____

_____

Three things I have to do today:

1) _____

_____

2) _____

_____

3) _____

_____

Three things I won't do today:

1) _____

_____

2) _____

_____

3) _____

_____

My soul is calling me to .....

Desire(s):

Inspired Action Step(s) I will take today:

Date: _____   M T W Th F S Su

:Ö: BREATHE   :Ö: HYDRATE   :Ö: MOVE   :Ö: SOUL CARE

Responsibility = Power

How I want to feel today:

_____

I am:

_____

Three things I'm grateful for:

1) _____

_____

2) _____

_____

3) _____

_____

Three things I love about myself:

1) _____

_____

2) _____

_____

3) _____

_____

Three things I have to do today:

1) _____

_____

2) _____

_____

3) _____

_____

Three things I won't do today:

1) _____

_____

2) _____

_____

3) _____

_____

My soul is calling me to .....

Desire(s):

_____
_____
_____

Inspired Action Step(s) I will take today:

_____
_____
_____

Weekly Soul Check

Describe how you felt this week in one word:

_____

If it was positive feeling, what can you do to feel that way more often?

_____

If it was a negative feeling, what can you do to feel more positive?

_____

What am I forcing?

_____

What am I allowing?

_____

What is one thing I will do less of?

_____

What is one thing I will do more of?

_____

What didn't work this week?

_____

I am releasing:

_____

I am calling in:

_____

Celebrate! What went well this week?

_____

Be still.

Silence the noise.

Let it be.

Choose again.

Savor the moments.

You are magic.

Responsibility = Power

Week Three

. . .

Expand

Weekly Intentions

Dates: _____

How do you want to feel this week? What are you going to be intentional about this week?

Shining	Glamorous	Clear
Feminine	Artistic	Relentless
Fearless	Energetic	Strong
Blessed	Radiant	Balanced
Whole	Determined	Zen
Revived	Blissful	Awakened

Weekly Challenge

Remove the Mask
Practice living more authenticity and get out of your comfort zone.

Part of soul care is being aware and honoring self... so today we are going to do just that. Just as you are. Part of it is also breaking through barriers and comfort zones. We can't gr ow or be aware if we are STUCK.

Do something different in your day to day.
Some suggestions are:

- Go without makeup.
- Wear a different shade than you normally would. Add a pop of color.
- Dress differently or style your hair differently.
- Go a different route to work, drop off, home...
- Have a conversation you need to have
- Reach out to someone you'd like to
- Say hi to a stranger
- Eat something you wouldn't normally eat
- Post a video and share something out of the ordinary with us.
- Post a video or a photo of you with no makeup on, or with a new shade of lipstick on...

Journal Prompts
What did you do? How did you feel? Will you make an effort to do this more often? What's the worst that you thought would happen?
How did you expect to feel?

Date: _____ M T W Th F S Su

BREATHE   HYDRATE   MOVE   SOUL CARE

Be intentional.

How I want to feel today:

_____

I am:

_____

Three things I'm grateful for:

1) _____
_____
2) _____
_____
3) _____
_____

Three things I love about myself:

1) _____
_____
2) _____
_____
3) _____
_____

Three things I have to do today:

1) _____
_____
2) _____
_____
3) _____
_____

Three things I won't do today:

1) _____
_____
2) _____
_____
3) _____
_____

My soul is calling me to .....

Desire(s):

_____

_____

_____

Inspired Action Step(s) I will take today:

_____

_____

_____

Free Write...

Date: _____ M T W Th F S Su

☼ BREATHE   ☼ HYDRATE   ☼ MOVE   ☼ SOUL CARE

You are glorious.

How I want to feel today:

_____

I am:

_____

Three things I'm grateful for:

1) _____

_____

2) _____

_____

3) _____

_____

Three things I love about myself:

1) _____

_____

2) _____

_____

3) _____

_____

Three things I have to do today:

1) _____

_____

2) _____

_____

3) _____

_____

Three things I won't do today:

1) _____

_____

2) _____

_____

3) _____

_____

My soul is calling me to .....

Desire(s):

_____

_____

_____

Inspired Action Step(s) I will take today:

_____

_____

_____

Date: _____ M T W Th F S Su

☼ BREATHE   ☼ HYDRATE   ☼ MOVE   ☼ SOUL CARE

Blessings abound.

How I want to feel today:

_____

I am:

_____

Three things I'm grateful for:

1) _____

_____

2) _____

_____

3) _____

_____

Three things I love about myself:

1) _____

_____

2) _____

_____

3) _____

_____

Three things I have to do today:

1) _____

_____

2) _____

_____

3) _____

_____

Three things I won't do today:

1) _____

_____

2) _____

_____

3) _____

_____

My soul is calling me to .....

Desire(s):

_____
_____
_____

Inspired Action Step(s) I will take today:

_____
_____
_____

Date: _____ M T W Th F S Su

:Ö: BREATHE   :Ö: HYDRATE   :Ö: MOVE   :Ö: SOUL CARE

The answer is in the surrender.

How I want to feel today:

_____

I am:

_____

Three things I'm grateful for:

1) _____
   _____
2) _____
   _____
3) _____
   _____

Three things I love about myself:

1) _____
   _____
2) _____
   _____
3) _____
   _____

Three things I have to do today:

1) _____
   _____
2) _____
   _____
3) _____
   _____

Three things I won't do today:

1) _____
   _____
2) _____
   _____
3) _____
   _____

My soul is calling me to.....

Desire(s):

_____
_____
_____
_____

Inspired Action Step(s) I will take today:

_____
_____
_____
_____

Free Write

Date: _____ M T W Th F S Su

☼ BREATHE   ☼ HYDRATE   ☼ MOVE   ☼ SOUL CARE

Feed your soul.

How I want to feel today:

_____

I am:

_____

Three things I'm grateful for:

1) _____
   _____
2) _____
   _____
3) _____
   _____

Three things I love about myself:

1) _____
   _____
2) _____
   _____
3) _____
   _____

Three things I have to do today:

1) _____
   _____
2) _____
   _____
3) _____
   _____

Three things I won't do today:

1) _____
   _____
2) _____
   _____
3) _____
   _____

My soul is calling me to .....

Desire(s):

_____

_____

_____

Inspired Action Step(s) I will take today:

_____

_____

_____

Free Write

Free Write

Date: _____ M T W Th F S Su

☼ BREATHE   ☼ HYDRATE   ☼ MOVE   ☼ SOUL CARE

Listen to the pull.

How I want to feel today:

_____

I am:

_____

Three things I'm grateful for:

1) _____

_____

2) _____

_____

3) _____

_____

Three things I love about myself:

1) _____

_____

2) _____

_____

3) _____

_____

Three things I have to do today:

1) _____

_____

2) _____

_____

3) _____

_____

Three things I won't do today:

1) _____

_____

2) _____

_____

3) _____

_____

My soul is calling me to .....

Desire(s):

_____
_____
_____

Inspired Action Step(s) I will take today:

_____
_____
_____

Date: _____ M T W Th F S Su

☀ BREATHE   ☀ HYDRATE   ☀ MOVE   ☀ SOUL CARE

Own your voice.

How I want to feel today:

_____

I am:

_____

Three things I'm grateful for:

1) _____
   _____
2) _____
   _____
3) _____
   _____

Three things I love about myself:

1) _____
   _____
2) _____
   _____
3) _____
   _____

Three things I have to do today:

1) _____
   _____
2) _____
   _____
3) _____
   _____

Three things I won't do today:

1) _____
   _____
2) _____
   _____
3) _____
   _____

My soul is calling me to .....

Desire(s):

_____

_____

_____

Inspired Action Step(s) I will take today:

_____

_____

_____

Free Write

Free Write

Weekly Soul Check

Describe how you felt this week in one word:

_____

If it was positive feeling, what can you do to feel that way more often?

_____

If it was a negative feeling, what can you do to feel more positive?

_____

What am I forcing?

_____

What am I allowing?

_____

What is one thing I will do less of?

_____

What is one thing I will do more of?

_____

What didn't work this week?

_____

I am releasing:

_____

I am calling in:

_____

Celebrate! What went well this week?

_____

Be intentional.

You are glorious.

Blessings abound.

The answer is in the surrender.

Feed your soul.

Listen to the pull.

Own your voice.

Week Four
...
Shine Bright

Weekly Intentions

Dates: _____

How do you want to feel this week? What are you going to be intentional about this week?

Held	Creative	Safe
Appreciated	Hopeful	Spontaneous
Happy	Positive	Radiant
Clear	Guided	Courageous
Free	Present	Passionate
Replenished	Enough	Connected

Weekly Challenge

Move Your Body

This week's challenge is focused moving your body. Moving your body daily has a number of health benefits and is great for overall mind, body & soul wellness. It gets the energy flowing and brings in high vibes.

Suggestions:

- Dance party! Put on your favorite tunes & shake it out!
- Attend a group fitness, yoga or dance class. Don't worry about long term commitment, just do what feels good this week.
- Go for a jog or a walk outdoors. You'll be amazed what the fresh air will do for you!
- Work out at home. You can find tons of workouts online that require little room and equipment that are still efficient and fun!

Journal Prompts:
What did you do? How did you feel? Will you make an effort move more often?

Date: _____ M T W Th F S Su

☼ BREATHE   ☼ HYDRATE   ☼ MOVE   ☼ SOUL CARE

Be the light.

How I want to feel today:

_____

I am:

_____

Three things I'm grateful for:

1) _____
   _____
2) _____
   _____
3) _____
   _____

Three things I love about myself:

1) _____
   _____
2) _____
   _____
3) _____
   _____

Three things I have to do today:

1) _____
   _____
2) _____
   _____
3) _____
   _____

Three things I won't do today:

1) _____
   _____
2) _____
   _____
3) _____
   _____

My soul is calling me to .....

Desire(s):

_____

_____

_____

_____

Inspired Action Step(s) I will take today:

_____

_____

_____

_____

Free Write

Free Write

Date: _____ M T W Th F S Su

☼ BREATHE   ☼ HYDRATE   ☼ MOVE   ☼ SOUL CARE

Rise up.

How I want to feel today:

_____

I am:

_____

Three things I'm grateful for:

1) _____
   _____
2) _____
   _____
3) _____
   _____

Three things I love about myself:

1) _____
   _____
2) _____
   _____
3) _____
   _____

Three things I have to do today:

1) _____
   _____
2) _____
   _____
3) _____
   _____

Three things I won't do today:

1) _____
   _____
2) _____
   _____
3) _____
   _____

My soul is calling me to.....

Desire(s):

_____

_____

_____

Inspired Action Step(s) I will take today:

_____

_____

_____

Free Write

Date: _____ M T W Th F S Su

☀ BREATHE   ☀ HYDRATE   ☀ MOVE   ☀ SOUL CARE

No more playing small.

How I want to feel today:

_____

I am:

_____

Three things I'm grateful for:

1) _____
   _____
2) _____
   _____
3) _____
   _____

Three things I love about myself:

1) _____
   _____
2) _____
   _____
3) _____
   _____

Three things I have to do today:

1) _____
   _____
2) _____
   _____
3) _____
   _____

Three things I won't do today:

1) _____
   _____
2) _____
   _____
3) _____
   _____

My soul is calling me to.....

Desire(s):

_____
_____
_____

Inspired Action Step(s) I will take today:

_____
_____
_____

Date: _____ M T W Th F S Su

☼ BREATHE   ☼ HYDRATE   ☼ MOVE   ☼ SOUL CARE

Begin where you are.

How I want to feel today:

_____

I am:

_____

Three things I'm grateful for:

1) _____
   _____
2) _____
   _____
3) _____
   _____

Three things I love about myself:

1) _____
   _____
2) _____
   _____
3) _____
   _____

Three things I have to do today:

1) _____
   _____
2) _____
   _____
3) _____
   _____

Three things I won't do today:

1) _____
   _____
2) _____
   _____
3) _____
   _____

My soul is calling me to .....

Desire(s):

Inspired Action Step(s) I will take today:

Free Write

Date: _____ M T W Th F S Su

☼ BREATHE   ☼ HYDRATE   ☼ MOVE   ☼ SOUL CARE

Release expectations.

How I want to feel today:

_____

I am:

_____

Three things I'm grateful for:

1) _____
   _____
2) _____
   _____
3) _____
   _____

Three things I love about myself:

1) _____
   _____
2) _____
   _____
3) _____
   _____

Three things I have to do today:

1) _____
   _____
2) _____
   _____
3) _____
   _____

Three things I won't do today:

1) _____
   _____
2) _____
   _____
3) _____
   _____

My soul is calling me to .....

Desire(s):

Inspired Action Step(s) I will take today:

Free Write

Date: _____ M T W Th F S Su

☼ BREATHE   ☼ HYDRATE   ☼ MOVE   ☼ SOUL CARE

What is for me will not pass me.

How I want to feel today:

_____

I am:

_____

Three things I'm grateful for:

1) _____
   _____
2) _____
   _____
3) _____
   _____

Three things I love about myself:

1) _____
   _____
2) _____
   _____
3) _____
   _____

Three things I have to do today:

1) _____
   _____
2) _____
   _____
3) _____
   _____

Three things I won't do today:

1) _____
   _____
2) _____
   _____
3) _____
   _____

My soul is calling me to .....

Desire(s):

_____

_____

_____

_____

Inspired Action Step(s) I will take today:

_____

_____

_____

Free Write

Date: _____ M T W Th F S Su

☀ BREATHE   ☀ HYDRATE   ☀ MOVE   ☀ SOUL CARE

Live your passion.

How I want to feel today:

_____

I am:

_____

Three things I'm grateful for:

1) _____

2) _____

3) _____

Three things I love about myself:

1) _____

2) _____

3) _____

Three things I have to do today:

1) _____

2) _____

3) _____

Three things I won't do today:

1) _____

2) _____

3) _____

My soul is calling me to.....

Desire(s):

_____

_____

_____

Inspired Action Step(s) I will take today:

_____

_____

_____

Weekly Soul Check

Describe how you felt this week in one word:

_____

If it was positive feeling, what can you do to feel that way more often?

_____

If it was a negative feeling, what can you do to feel more positive?

_____

What am I forcing?

_____

What am I allowing?

_____

What is one thing I will do less of?

_____

What is one thing I will do more of?

_____

What didn't work this week?

_____

I am releasing:

_____

I am calling in:

_____

Celebrate! What went well this week?

_____

Be the light.

Rise up.

No more playing small.

Begin where you are.

Release expectations.

What is for me will not
pass me.

Live your passion.

I Am
...
Creative Affirmation Pages

I AM

CALM

&

IN CONTROL

OF MY

THOUGHTS.

I AM FOCUSED ON MY BREATH & I AM BREATHING DEEPLY.

I AM
A MAGNET
FOR
WONDERFUL
THINGS.

I
RELEASE
EXPECTATIONS
&
GIVE
MYSELF
GRACE.

I am abundant.

I AM
CAPABLE OF
HANDLING
ANY
CHALLENGE
THAT COMES
MY WAY.

I AM
BLESSED.

I BREATHE IN

CONFIDENCE

&

BREATHE OUT

FEAR.

I AM
RELAXED
&
CALM.

I am strong & will overcome.

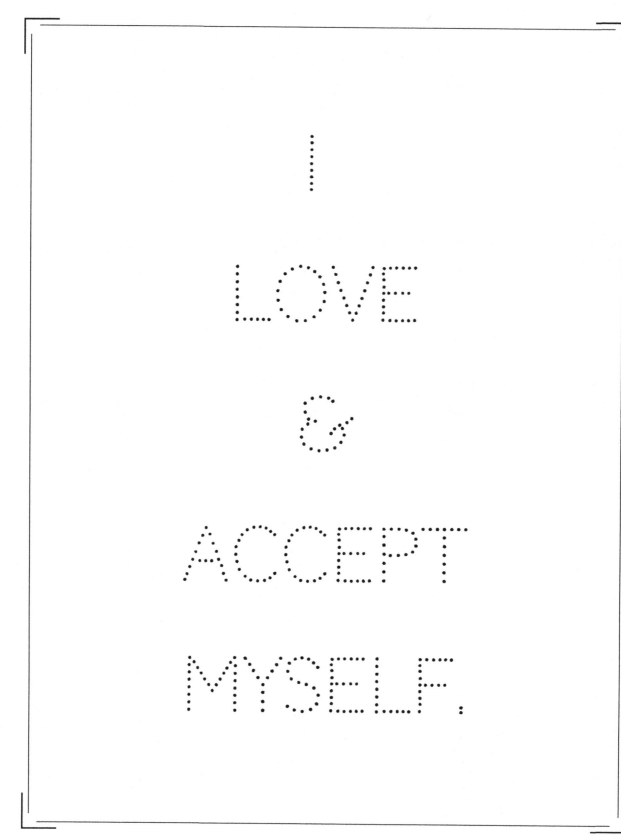

I
LOVE
&
ACCEPT
MYSELF.

I AM

SAFE.

I AM

AT

PEACE.

I AM FREE OF ANXIETY & I AM LIVING A CALM LIFE.

I have everything I need within me & above me.

I AM
DESERVING
OF
HAPPY
THOUGHTS.

I AM ATTRACTING POSITIVE ENERGY INTO MY BODY.

I AM

LOVED,

LOVING

&

LOVABLE.

I AM
GRATEFUL.

I am making a positive impact on the world.

I AM

HEALTHY

&

STRONG.

I TRUST MYSELF, MY HEART & MY SOUL.

I MAKE TIME FOR MYSELF & THINGS THAT SET MY SOUL ON FIRE.

I ASK FOR WHAT I WANT.

Life happens for me, not to me.

I

CHOOSE

POSITIVE

THOUGHTS.

I RELEASE
MY PAST
&
ENJOY
THE NOW.

I LET GO

OF THINGS

I CANNOT

CONTROL.

I CREATE MY REALITY.

I am

worthy.

Clear the Clutter

&

Free Your Soul Challenge

Unfollow anyone or any page on social media that makes you feel stressed, anxious, angry or less than. Do this as often as necessary.

 Unsubscribe to any emails that don't serve you, that you don't read, or that are taking up space in your inbox and mind!

 Challenge yourself to be 100 percent present with your family, spouse, friends for at least 1 hour today. Put your phone on airplane mode.
Breathe in the moments.

 Delete any text messages, group messages or threads that don't serve you.

 Release FOMO (fear of missing out). Trust that you will not miss out on anything. Everything is divine. Everything is happening FOR you and right on time.

 Take 10 minutes & a trash bag around your house - discard any trash, broken toys, broken knick knacks, unused toiletries, empty bottles, anything that is not serving you or is taking up space & energy. *Dig deeper* - trash everything that triggers painful memories, that doesn't fit or doesn't make you feel empowered.

 Create a budget - there are dozens of apps or spreadsheet software & templates that can help you create this.

 Make a list of appointments and calls you need to make.
Make at least one daily for the next five days.
Do the one you dread most first.

 Stop worrying about what other people think about you. Stop making decisions based off of how it will affect them. (within reason of course) but when it comes to your life, LIVE IT!

Read the books as your soul leads you to read.
Don't read just to check off a "personal development" box.

 Have a guilt free self care ritual in place to do once a week, once a month or once a day. (get your nails done, take a relaxing bath, get a massage, hang in your hammock, grab a fancy coffee or tea, go to a wine tasting)

 Nourish the relationships that mean the most to you.
Say what you'll do and do what you say.

 Don't gossip. It only lowers your vibe and accomplishes nothing. Journal out your feelings instead. By doing this, you can see what is triggering you and what is a mirror about that particular person or situation.
When you discover that, you can heal.

 When you feel fearful, write it down. Name it. Ask yourself why you are feeling fear around this topic. What is one thing you can do to move toward it and away from the fear?

 Own it. Take responsibility for your actions and reactions. Feel through the feelings and allow yourself to feel them. Ask yourself why you're feeling this way and release any shame or guilt about it. Then replace with a positive thought and feeling.

 Stop trying to be everything to everyone. We are all good at certain things, in our own way. Cultivate those things. Set boundaries for people who don't respect your feelings and thoughts and keep your healthy distance.

 Pay it forward. Do something nice for someone just because. Release any attachments, outcomes and rewards. Do it just because.

 Build a feel good playlist. Save it to your favorites and turn it up often!

Feel free to use this space for your own clear the clutter ideas,
to-do's and to-don't's, doodles, and thoughts.

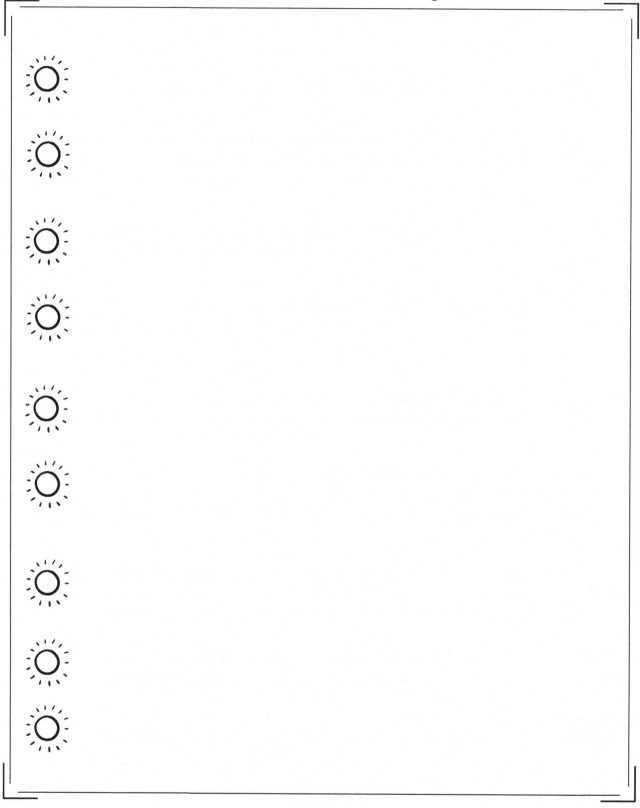

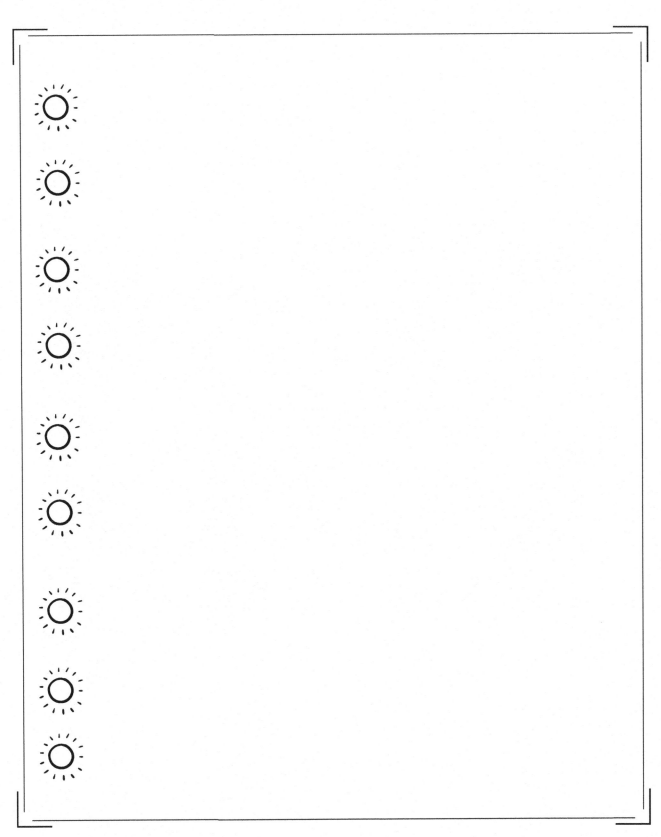

Dig Deep

...

Journal Prompts

Date: _____ M T W Th F S Su

Do you like who you are becoming? Why or why not?

Date: _____ M T W Th F S Su

Who are you when you are most proud?
Did you live up to that today?
If not, what will you do moving forward
to make yourself proud?

What makes you feel like a child again?
How often are you practicing doing these things?
How can you integrate more of these things into your life?

What is one thing you have been through that you
thought you'd never get through?
How does it feel knowing you made it through?

What are you holding on to?
What is stopping you from letting it go?

Date: _____ M T W Th F S Su

What is your biggest fear & why?
When you feel fear, where do you feel it in your body?

Where in your life are you overcommitted?
What is one thing you can take off your plate today
to relieve stress, anxiety, overwhelm, frustration?

What do you love about the people you admire most?
Do you recognize these aspects within yourself?
Why or why not?

List 10 things that you love most about yourself. Dig deep.

Date: _____ M T W Th F S Su

How is your soul?

Date: _____ M T W Th F S Su

Do you believe you are worthy of anything you want in this life? Why or why not?

What lights you up?
What dims your shine?

Date: _____ M T W Th F S Su

What advice would you give your younger self?

What scares you right now?
What is the worst that could happen?
What is the best thing that could happen?

Date: _____ M T W Th F S Su

If you could change one thing about your life, what would it be?
What is one thing you can do today to make
or move toward that change?

Who are you?
What is the story?
Where do you see yourself in five years?

Date: _____ M T W Th F S Su

What is the first thing you think of when you
go to sleep & when you wake up?
Are you willing to take a leap of faith & inspired action
steps to make it happen? Why or why not?
What is one thing you can do today to move you closer to that?

What is one thing that you have that you often take for granted? What is one thing you can do today to get in a state of gratitude for it?

In what ways do you judge others?
Do you see how it is comparable to how you judge yourself?
How? Rewrite those judgements & forgive yourself.

Date: _____ M T W Th F S Su

What grounds you?
Do you practice this often? Why or why not?
What is one thing you can do to feel more grounded today?

Date: _____ M T W Th F S Su

What is something about you that you hold back on
telling people about yourself? (Shames / fears / thoughts?) Why?
What will it take to break free from the hold it has on you?
What can you do today to share more of you?

What passion/thing/cause do you find yourself talking about daily? Are you committed to bringing more light to that passion? How?

If you could go anywhere, where would it be?
Why? How can you make that a reality?
What is one step, right now that you can take to bring you closer?

Date: _____ M T W Th F S Su

What do you want more than anything?
What is one thing you can do today to get closer to that thing?

Date: _____ M T W Th F S Su

How have you been playing small?
Why do you think this is?
What can you let go of right this moment that will
allow you to grow, think bigger & play bigger?

Date: _____ M T W Th F S Su

How have you been unkind to yourself?
What is one thing you can do to be more kind to yourself today?

Date: _____ M T W Th F S Su

When do you feel most like you?
What are you doing? Who are you with?
Visualize it & write it out in detail here.

Date: _____ M T W Th F S Su

What are 10 things you are grateful for right this moment?

Date: _____ M T W Th F S Su

Are you joyful?
List three things that you will do today
to bring more joy into your life.

Date: _____ M T W Th F S Su

Make a list of resentments, grudges, & limiting
beliefs or stories you carry that hold you back in some way.
How can you release, forgive &/or rewrite those now?
How does it feel to release & forgive?

Resources & What's Next

Email
thesoulshinecollective@gmail.com

Website
www.thesoulshinecollective.com

Self-Paced Online Courses
https://thesoulshinecollective.com/11-coaching/self-paced-courses/

1:1 Coaching
https://thesoulshinecollective.com/11-coaching/

Photography Prints Available
https://thesoulshinecollective.com/shop-2/

Portrait Experiences
https://thesoulshinecollective.com/coaching/photography-experiences/

Collaborations & Workshops
Email thesoulshinecollective@gmail.com

Further Journaling Resources
https://thesoulshinecollective.com/11-coaching/self-paced-courses/
5-day-journaling-challenge/

Thank You!

I am beyond honored to have been a small part
in your journey through this creative guide.
I pray that it served your soul in ways beyond your
wildest dreams and brought clarity, intention & flow
into your life where you needed it.

Blessings, love & light to you always!

- Amy